IMAGES
of America

WADMALAW
ISLAND

IMAGES
of America

WADMALAW
ISLAND

Michelle Adams and Kate Di Silvestre

ARCADIA
PUBLISHING

Published by Arcadia Publishing
Charleston, South Carolina

Library of Congress Control Number: 2012938566

For all general information, please contact Arcadia Publishing:
Telephone 843-853-2070
Fax 843-853-0044
E-mail sales@arcadiapublishing.com
For customer service and orders:
Toll-Free 1-888-313-2665

Visit us on the Internet at www.arcadiapublishing.com

CONTENTS

ACKNOWLEDGMENTS

Many thanks to Jane Knight and Bryn Riley at the Charleston Tea Plantation for allowing us access to their archives and for the numerous questions answered and photographs scanned. Thank you to Bertha Middleton for personally showing me around the Wadmalaw Community Center and for contributing so many photographs. I would also like to give thanks to James Burton of Camp Ho Non Wah for answering many questions over the months and contributing just as many photographs. And many thanks to Lish Thompson, who was instrumental during the development of this book.

Kate would like to thank her family and friends who offered their support and patience while completing this project—specifically, her wonderful parents; siblings Megan, Robby, and Joey; and Mom Mom and Grandaddy. Thank you to Jordan for driving her up and down Wadmalaw more times than can be counted and for the help and support he provided every day.

Michelle would like to thank her family for their continued support—especially her children, Amanda and Bonham, for being patient while Mommy worked.

INTRODUCTION

The island of Wadmalaw has remained largely unchanged for the last 300 years. The drone of the cicadas is still the only sound often heard in the deep heat of summer. Small housing communities and farms continue to be the only inhabitants of the island. One lone grocery store marks the entrance of commercialism to the island along with two plantations that evolved their working production of tea and wine into tourist destinations. And one weekend of the year, the little town of Rockville's population swells from an influx of happy partygoers. The island is truly a unique visit back in time that is rarely found these days.

Wadmalaw was first inhabited by the Cusabo Indians, a combination of several tribes: Kiawah, Ashepoo, Bohicketts, Edistow, Escamacus, and Stono. Wolves, deer, cougars, snakes, alligators, and wild boar roamed the island long before the arrival of the Europeans. Eventually, the white man arrived and changed the island forever. After Charles II regained his throne from Oliver Cromwell, he granted the Carolina territory to eight of his loyal friends, the Lords Proprietors. The first settlement the Lords Proprietors were able to arrange was that of Charles Towne. The settlement was established on the west bank of the Ashley River in 1670 and was later moved to its current location on the peninsula in 1680, where the settlers could better defend themselves. The town, originally known as Charles Towne, was soon to become a large port and the settlement eventually expanded beyond the walled city of the original plan. Capt. Robert Sandford and the crew of the Berkeley Bay landed on the island in June 1666. He and his crew encountered Wadmalaw Island after a trip up the Bohicket Creek, and he is believed to have landed where today's Rockville now resides. Captain Sandford claimed the land for England and for the Lords Proprietors.

The Lords Proprietors then divided up the available land to settlers to develop handing out land grants to those willing to make the properties successful. Wadmalaw was also divided this way; thus, the Wadmalaw plantations were established to grow staple crops such as sea island cotton, indigo, and rice. Charles Towne was the entrance point for African slaves imported into the United States. The port of Charles Towne was the main dropping point for Africans captured and transported into the United States for sale as slaves, and 40 percent of slaves imported into the United States came through the Port of Charleston. Slaves who lived on sea island plantations such as Wadmalaw were able to create a language and culture that is today known as Gullah.

The Gullah people were able to preserve much of their African culture due to geography, climate, and patterns of importation of enslaved Africans. Imported from the western coast of Africa, these slaves were sold to the slave owners in what was then Charles Towne, South Carolina. By the middle of the 18th century, rice had become a successful cash crop in South Carolina and Georgia. This was due to the African farmers that brought the skills for cultivation and tidal irrigation to make rice one of the most successful industries in early America.

The subtropical climate of the South Carolina and Georgia coast, or the Lowcountry, created the ideal condition for successful rice production but also made it vulnerable to malaria and yellow fever. Slaves were more resistant to these diseases, having acquired some immunity in Africa. Often, the white planters would escape to a seaside village to escape these virulent illnesses and the dreaded summer heat. Wadmalaw soon saw the rise of a little town called Rockville, where many of the plantation families went during the summer months.

The Gullah culture continued to be infused with additional slaves brought into the plantation as laborers as the rice industry expanded. Because planters devoted large areas of land to plantations for rice and indigo, the white population of the Lowcountry and sea islands grew at a slower rate than the black population. In addition, the white population of the sea islands grew at a slower pace due to the fear of these diseases and the large areas that plantations covered. Because planters devoted large areas of land to plantations for rice and indigo, the white population of the Lowcountry and sea islands grew at a slower rate than the black population. By about 1708, South Carolina had a black majority.

The white planters left overseers, or black "drivers," in charge of the plantations. This allowed the large African workforces, which were often reinforced with more workers from the same regions of Africa, the ability to develop a culture based in elements of African language and culture. These slaves differed greatly from the slaves in Virginia and North Carolina who had more interaction with white people and lived in smaller communities.

Another successful but short-lived crop was indigo. It was first introduced to South Carolina in 1739 and became a successful cash crop by an enterprising young lady named Eliza Lucas Pinckney. Her father, the governor of Antigua, sent Eliza seeds to see which would be suited for the Carolina climate. After several attempts, she had her first successful shipment of indigo to England in 1747, and it became a staple crop from South Carolina until the Revolutionary War. During the war, more attention was paid to rice production. After the war, South Carolina could not compete with the cheaper and better quality of indigo coming from India. By the end of the 18th century, cotton had taken over indigo's place as an important export.

Sea island cotton, a unique strain of cotton found in the Lowcountry, was another successful cash crop for many of the local families. Sea island cotton boasts extra-long fibers that became very desired. It was first introduced in Hilton Head by William Elliott in 1790. Sea island cotton produced a higher-quality cotton than was previously seen in the America. It made many planters, including those on Wadmalaw, very wealthy. Grown on the sea islands of South Carolina and Georgia, this strain of cotton served as an important part of the Beaufort economy. Beaufort became the wealthiest and most cultured town of its size in America because of the sea island cotton crop.

During the Civil War, many planters removed their slaves and headed upstate. Some slaves were able to escape and many made it north or to Hilton Head or Beaufort where Union troops were stationed. Early in the war, the South knew that it could not defend the sea islands and abandoned them to the Union troops. When the slaves reached the Union troops, some were enlisted in a black regiment and fought against the South.

After the Civil War, planters returned to their land and tried to rebuild. Wadmalaw was no different and life resumed a little differently than before. Many planters turned to the sharecropper system and allowed their former slaves to remain on their plantations in return for a share of the crops they raised. Little changed on the island and the slow-paced lives of the island continued on until 1890 when planters organized the first sailing regatta at Rockville. The Rockville Regatta has become a time honored tradition recently celebrated its 120th anniversary.

In the last century, Wadmalaw has also seen the development of two new crops to the island. The Lipton Tea Company began operating an experimental tea farm on Wadmalaw Island in 1960, and it was sold in 1987 to Mack Fleming and Bill Hall. Fleming and Hall converted the experimental farm into a working tea plantation known today as the Charleston Tea Plantation which utilizes a converted cotton picker and tobacco harvester to mechanically harvest its tea. The Charleston Tea Plantation was purchased in 2003 by the Bigelow Tea Company and now offers tours of the last remaining working tea farm in America. The other new crop to Wadmalaw is a sweet tea–flavored vodka called Firefly Vodka. Due to the recognizable flavor and its cultural significance, it is popular throughout the South.

Wadmalaw has endured the slow evolution that the entire South has experienced from the rise of cotton and rice to the economic devastation after the Civil War. It has also seen the introduction of new crops and a successful annual boat race. It also has uniquely remained one of the few undeveloped sea islands in the South. One truly steps back to a slower-paced time when visiting the island and finds it is possible to imagine life as it was in the past.

One

WADMALAW PLANTATIONS

Wadmalaw Island is a wonderful step back in time to a slower-paced lifestyle of plantations and cotton. Wadmalaw has undergone the same economical and historical events that the rest of the South has but has resisted commercial intrusion. No stores or gas stations can be found on the island, and it has retained the original sea island charm settlers fell in love with years ago. (Courtesy of the Charleston County Library.)

This plat for Yellow House plantation dates to 1855, though the earliest date of existence for this plantation is unknown. The plantation once covered 603 acres and had 43 slaves. At the time of this plat, the plantation was owned by Hugh Wilson. It was later owned by the Bryan family. (Courtesy of the South Carolina Department of Archives and History.)

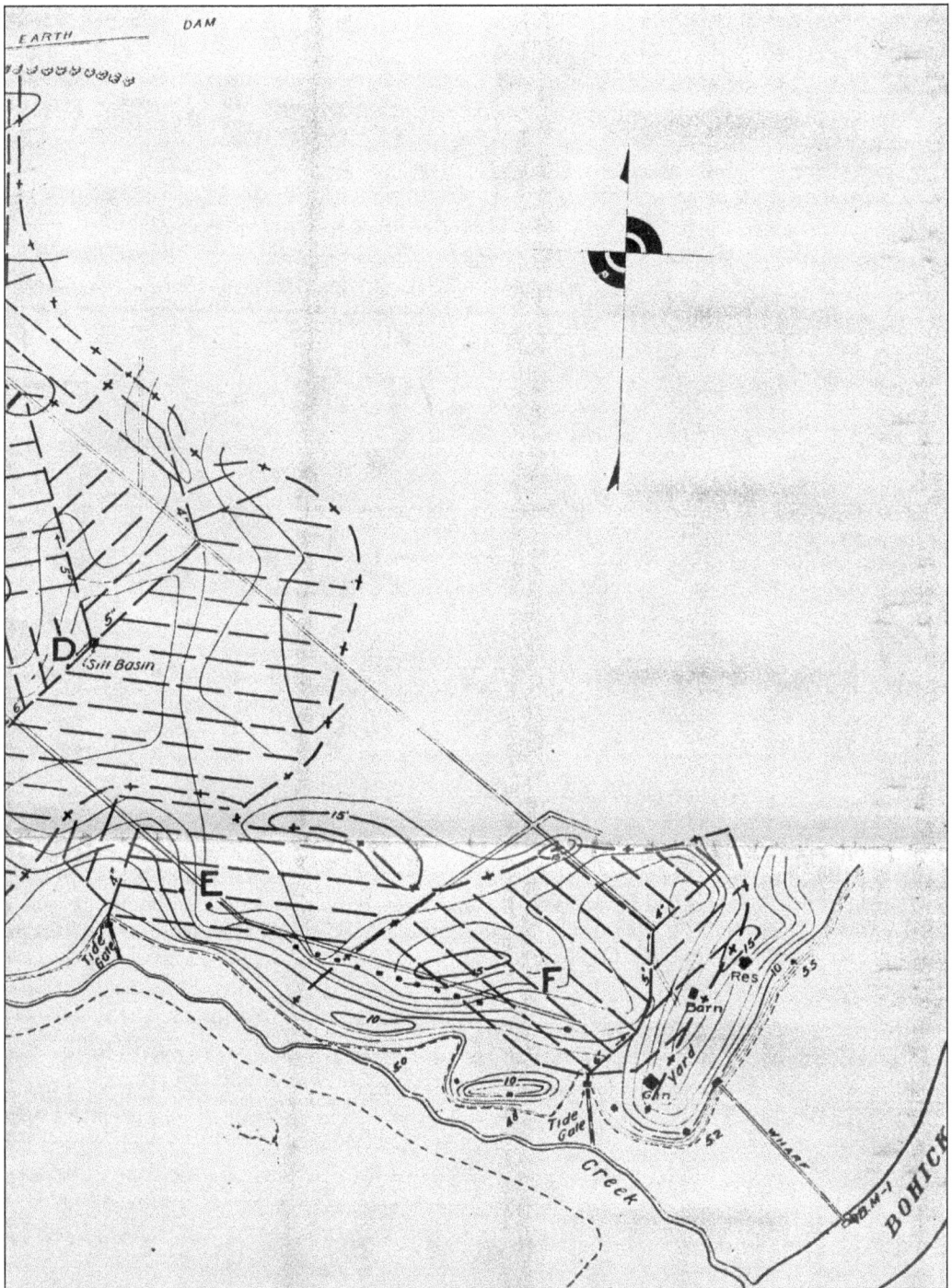

At different times throughout its history, Rosebank Plantation was owned by the Legare, McLeod, and Whitridge families. Rosebank Plantation is located on Bohicket Creek and can be dated back as far as 1821. It covered approximately 1,200 acres, and the primary crop was cotton. (Courtesy of the South Carolina Department of Archives and History.)

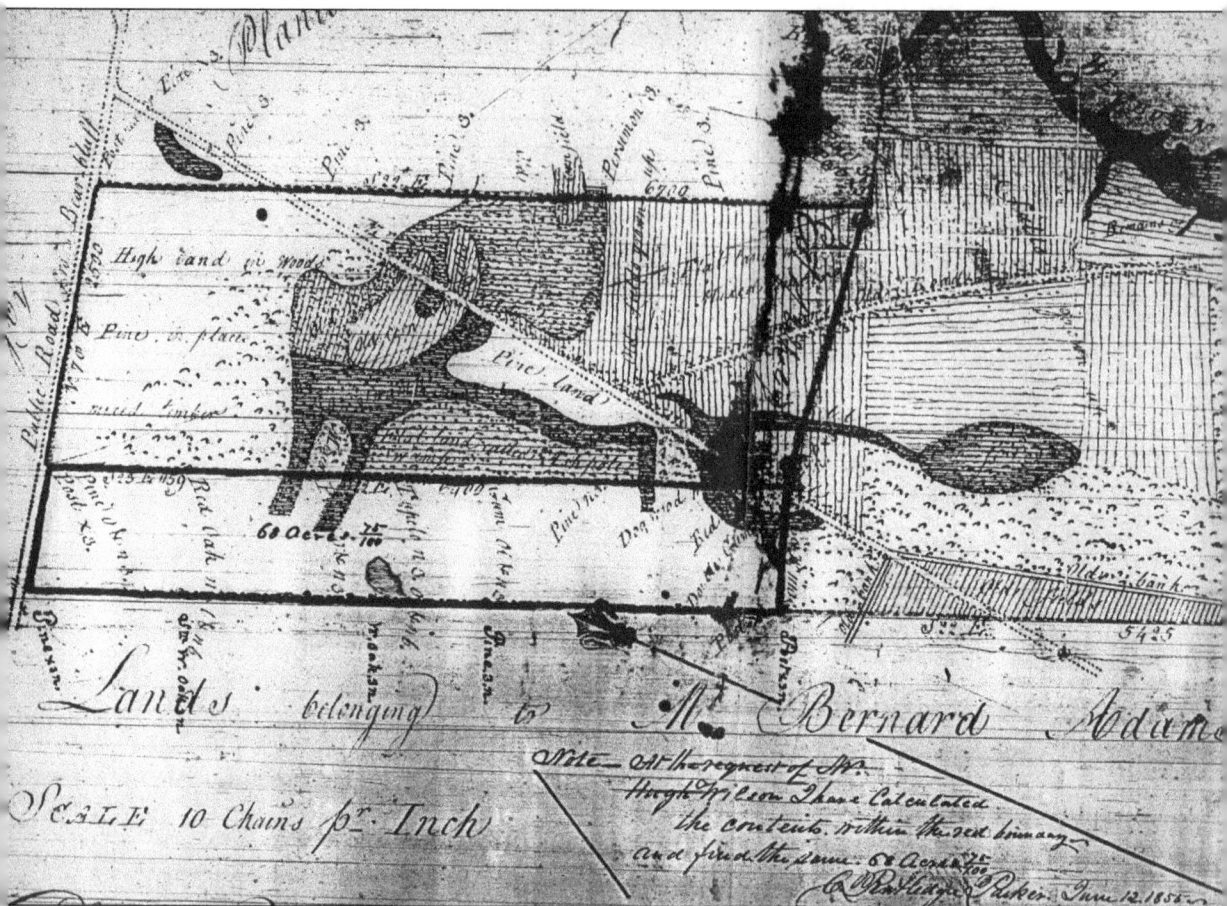

Bugby Plantation is located off Maybank Highway on Bugby Road along Bohicket Creek, a branch of the North Edisto River in St. John's Parish. Its earliest date of existence is 1840. It once encompassed 102 acres and had 26 slaves. The plantation was once owned by William Carson and the LaRoche, Townsend, Waight, and Wilson families. The Sosnowskis are the current owners. (Courtesy of the South Carolina Department of Archives and History.)

The estate inventory of Richard Jenkins, filed in April of 1857, lists the names of 150 slaves on the Jenkins plantation on Wadmalaw Island. The Jenkins family owned plantations on Wadmalaw Island and Edisto Island, all in Colleton and Charleston Counties in South Carolina. The Jenkins family owned Rackett Hall and Rockville Plantations on Wadmalaw and Brick House Plantation on Edisto Island. (Courtesy of the South Carolina Department of Archives and History.)

The Jenkins estate lists 150 slaves with mostly anglicized names such as Katy, Mary, Harry, and Molly. Often, these types of names were the result of the owner naming the slave children himself instead of allowing the slave parents that right. By 1857, it is also possible that the slaves have adopted the anglicized names of their owners and the other white people they encounter and have abandoned the names of their ancestors. (Courtesy of the South Carolina Department of Archives and History.)

This bill of sale shows the sale of a "Negro woman slave named Jenny" to Sarah Hutcherson of Wadmalaw Island from Joseph Lesson of Johns Island. The sale shows that Jenny was worth 400 pounds. From the amount listed, it is possible to guess that Jenny was a young woman, healthy, and possibly skilled as a cook or seamstress. (Courtesy of the South Carolina Department of Archives and History.)

State of South-Carolina.

Know all Men by these Presents, That I James Monk of Wadmalaw in the State aforesaid _____

for and in consideration of the sum of One hundred Pounds _____

to me in hand paid, at and before the sealing and delivery of these presents, By Marg.t E. Monk _____

the receipt whereof I do hereby acknowledge, to have bargained and sold, and by these presents do bargain, sell and deliver to the said Marg.t E Monk a negro wench named Jenny & her Child named Nanny & a negro fellow named Afton _____

TO HAVE AND TO HOLD the said Negroes with the future Issue & increase of the said female Slaves _____

unto the said Marg.t E Monk her _____

This bill of sale also lists the sale of a young woman named Jenny. James Monk of Wadmalaw Island sells "Margaret E. Monk a Negro wench named Jenny and her child named Nanny and Negro fellow named [the name is unreadable but starts with an A]". All are sold for 100 pounds. (Courtesy of the South Carolina Department of Archives and History.)

16

A true and perfect Inventory of the Goods, Chattels and Personal Estate of Margaret-Elizabeth Monk late of Wadmalaw Island Spinster deceased in the county of Colliton Made by Us whose names are hereunto subscribed as shewn unto Us by William Richard White Administrator to said Estate. ____

Jenny $300. Nanny $250. Sylvia $225. Moses $100. Nelly $150. ..... $ 1125. __.

1 Feather Bed, 1 Bolster &2 pillow $20. 1 Feather Bed, 1 Bolster & 1 Pillow $20. 1 Wooden Box 50 cents .... $ 40. 50

$1165. 50.

William Weston ___ Daniel Freer ___ Daniel Miscally ___ Josiah Rhodes ___

In Margaret E. Monk's estate record, Monk is listed as a spinster and as such has acquired a small household. In her estate list are two featherbeds, a bolster, pillows, a wooden box, and five slaves. In the list of slave names, Jenny and Nanny are still with her but the "Negro fellow" mentioned in the slave bill of sale is not. (Courtesy of the South Carolina Department of Archives and History.)

Know All Men by these Presents, That I Gilbert Chalmers of the City of Charleston in the State aforesaid _____

for and in consideration of the sum of Nine hundred & 06 Pounds Sterling _____

to him in hand paid, at and before the sealing and delivery of these presents, By Joseph Smilie Seabrook of Wadmalaw Island in the district of Charleston, in the State aforesaid _____

the receipt whereof I do hereby acknowledge, to have bargained and sold, and by these presents do bargain, sell and deliver to the said Joseph Smilie Seabrook the following Negro Slaves, to wit Sage & his Wife Darcus Jay and his Wife Sylvia, Tone & his Wife Rose, Lewis (or Leroy) & a Boy named Stephen — A Schooner called the Sophia & her Small Boat a Stock of Cattle marked C C Hogs &c &c _____

TO HAVE AND TO HOLD the said Negro Slaves Schooner & his small Boat, Stock of Cattle marked C C Stock of Hogs &c &c _____

unto the said Joseph Smilie Seabrook & His _____

Bills of sale would also mention married couples. This bill of sale to Joseph Seabrook of Wadmalaw Island mentions several couples, including "Sage and his wife Darcus, Jay and his wife Sylvia," as well as boy named Stephen and a schooner named the *Sophia*. (Courtesy of the South Carolina Department of Archives and History.)

374

in the Orig.

Mortgage
William Power
to
Henry Yonge.

This Indenture made the 23. day of March Anno Dom 1744/5 in the Eighteenth Year of the Reign of our Sovereign Lord George the Second by the Grace of God of Great Britain &c King Defender of the Faith &c **Between** William Power School=Master of Wadmelaw Island & Sarah his wife on the one part & Henry Yonge Surviving Partner of the Partnership lately Subsisting between Yonge & Wilkinson of Charles Town Store=keeper of the other part **Witnesseth** That for & in consideration of the sum of Five Hundred & fifty five pounds &c Currt money of South Carolina to the said William Power & Sarah his Wife in hand paid by the said Henry Yonge before the Ensealing & delivery of these presents, whereof they do hereby acknowledge the receipt & themselves well Content Satisfied & paid & thereof & of every part & parcell thereof doth hereby clearly & absolutely acquit, exonerate and discharge the said Henry Yonge his heirs, Exec.rs Adm.rs & assigns & every of them for ever by their presents, Hath Granted, Bargained & sold, & by these Presents doth Grant Bargain & sell unto the said Henry Yonge his Executors, Adm.rs & assigns, all that plantation or tract of land on Wadmelaw Island of him the said William Power & Sarah his wife Containing by Estimation One Hundred Acres butting & bounding as appears by a Deed of Gift of the same from Robert Cole & Mary his wife to their Son Micajah Cole bearing date the 30.th April Seventeen hundred & thirty three & is recorded in the Register's Office in Book T fol 163.164. and was by the said Micajah Cole left by Will to Sarah Spencer, now wife of William Power together with all & singular the Houses, Out houses, Edifices, Buildings, Rooms, Stables, Ways, Passages, waters, water courses, Lights, Easements, profits, Commodities, Emoluments, Appurtenances, & Hereditaments whatsoever to the said tract of Land & premises belonging in any wise appertaining, & the Reversion & Reversions, remainder & remainder Rents, Yearly & other rents & profits whatsoever of all & singular the said tract of Land & premises with their & every of their appurtenances before by these presents, Granted, Bargained & sold & every part & parcell

in the Orig.

This document is an indentured servant contract for a resident of Wadmalaw. Indentured servants were common in the colonies. A person would agree to work for a specific period of time in exchange for passage to the colonies. These workers included men, women, and children, mostly under the age of 21, who could not afford the passage and could not find work in the overcrowded labor markets of Europe. (Courtesy of the South Carolina Department of Archives and History.)

400 Acres
A Scale of 30 Chains

Bohicut Creek

Carolina Ss.

By virtue of a Warrant under the hand and Seal of Right Honble. Sir Nathaniel Johnson Knight and Governor Province to me directed dated the ninth day of March 1705 Caused to be admeasured and laid out to John Goble a tion Containing four hundred acres of Land or therea lying on Wadmelaw Island in Colleton County bou to the S. East on Bohicut Creek, to the N. East on Walkers Land to the N and N. West on James Youngs Walker and Christopher Harrisons Lands to the S. We John Stanyarne Land and hath such form and as are represented in a plat thereof here delineated and returned the tenth day of April In the Year 17 By me Thomas Broughton

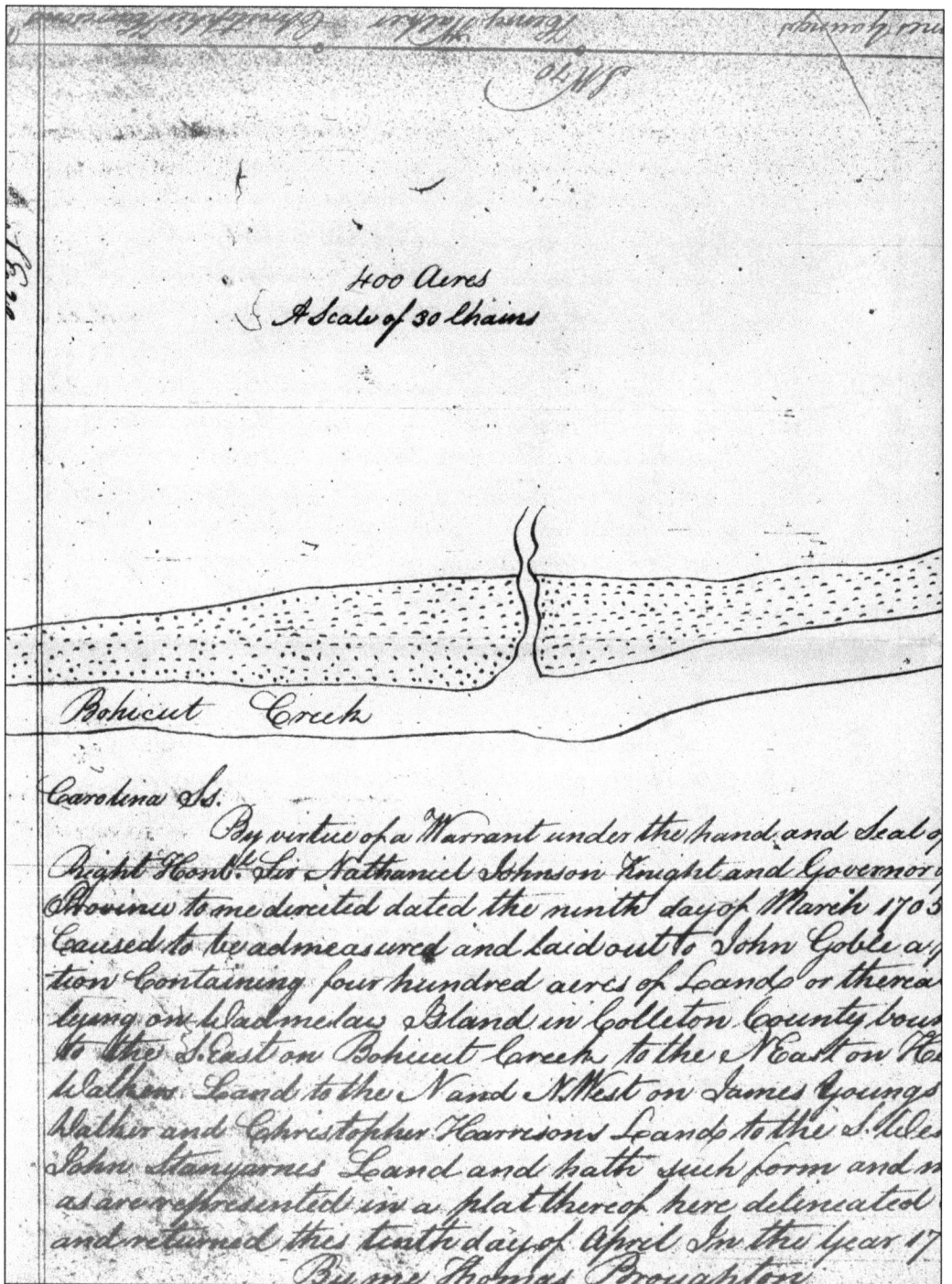

Most of these plats are measured by "chains." A chain is a unit of measurement that equals 66 feet or 22 yards. Ten chains also equal a furlong, and 80 chains equal one mile. An acre is measured by 10 square chains. The chain has been used for hundreds of years in England, and the practice was continued here in the colonies. (Courtesy of the South Carolina Department of Archives and History.)

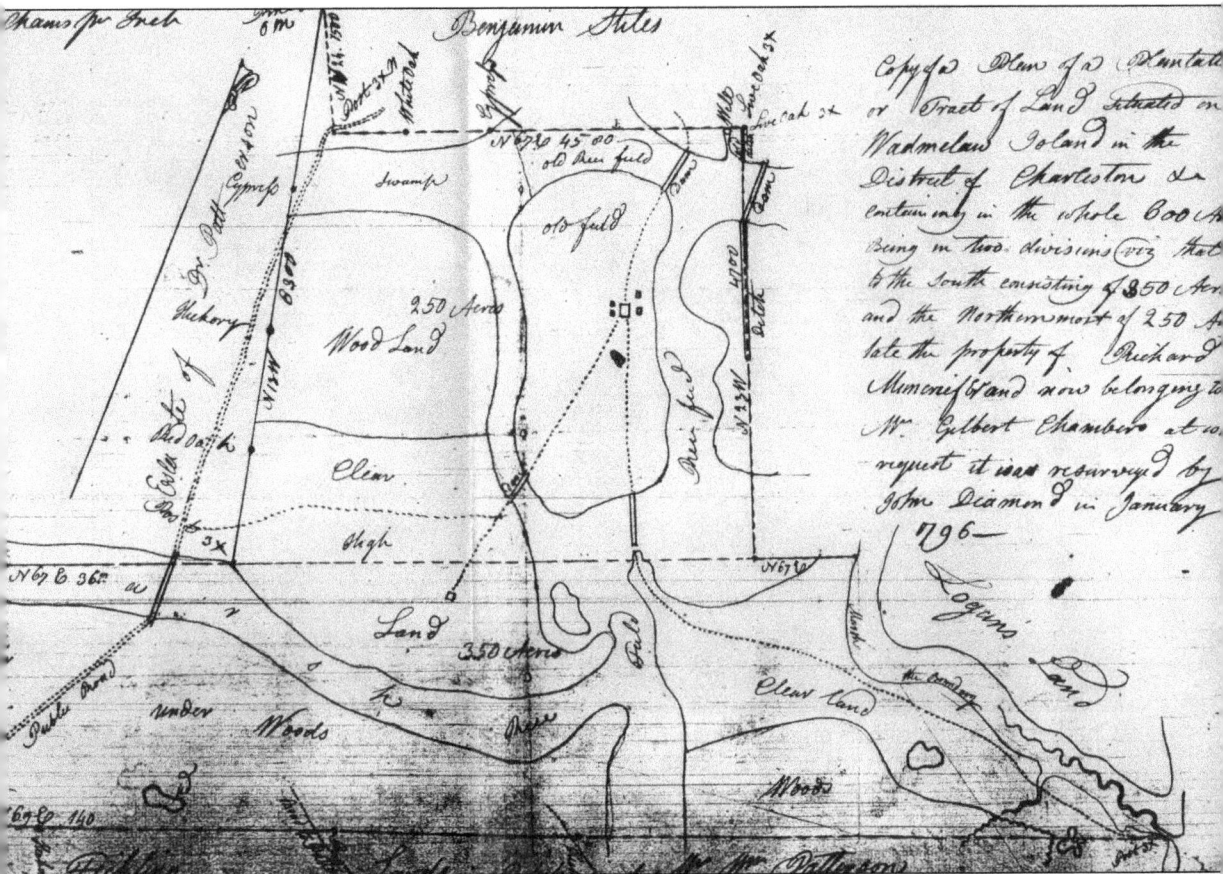

This tract of land is owned by Gilbert Chambers and contains 600 acres. The tract borders property owned by a Dr. Patterson and Benjamin Stiles. The tract shows areas of marshland, fields, ditches, and woodland. The tract comprises two properties—250 in the northern area and 350 in the southern area—that are now merged. (Courtesy of the South Carolina Department of Archives and History.)

Charleston moved from its original location in 1780 and had slowly grown from the initial walled city that had been planned by John Locke, then secretary to Lord Ashley Cooper, after whom the two rivers in Charleston are named. (Courtesy of the Library of Congress.)

As the city grew, so did its wealth, and the houses became larger with varied architecture. A unique style—the single house—became a common design. The Charleston single house is a one-room-wide structure with the narrow end of the house facing the street. Two-story verandas, called piazzas, stretch down the long side. (Courtesy of the Library of Congress.)

Slaves in the city had a different experience from those enslaved on isolated plantations, where more limited exposure to whites meant that African culture and language had a better chance of being preserved. (Courtesy of the Library of Congress.)

Often, homes in the city imitated plantation life. Many of the necessities of day-to-day life were contained within the high walls surrounding the main house and its dependencies. Food not able to be grown in a small garden either would have been brought in from the family plantation or purchased in town. (Courtesy of the Library of Congress.)

Neighboring islands housed the plantations of family members, as kinfolk often lived close by. This plantation belonged to the Seabrook family on Edisto Island. Members of this family could be found on many of the plantations that dotted the landscape throughout Charleston, including Wadmalaw Island. (Courtesy of the Library of Congress.)

Oak Grove Plantation is located on Leadenwah Creek, a branch of the North Edisto River on Wadmalaw Island. The plantation dates back to 1767, had 700 slaves, and grew rice. Benjamin Stiles owned the plantation in 1795. The plantation was also owned by the Bailey, Leigh, Noisette, and Porcher families over the years. (Courtesy of Daisy Leland.)

Two

PLANTATION LIFE

As early as 1680, South Carolina was growing rice successfully. By the early 18th century, the slave system had been established on a large scale and rice was the major export crop of the region. Rice had become extremely profitable, with Charleston rice exports rising from 10,000 pounds in 1698 to over 20 million pounds by 1730. South Carolina's tidal swamps were ideal for growing rice and indigo. (Courtesy of the Library of Congress.)

Slaves from the West Indies as well as West Africa helped carve out rice fields from tidal swamps found along South Carolina's coast. Slaves cleared the low-lying land of huge cypress and gum trees and created canals, dikes, and trunks (small floodgates) that flooded and then drained the field with the high and low tides. Through the Civil War, plantation owners became wealthy while slaves did the backbreaking work of planting, tending, and harvested the rice. (Courtesy of the Library of Congress.)

Between 1783 and the early 1800s, the coastal Southeast was transformed by the onset of rice cultivation and its use of the tidal flow method. Though this method was only practical for a small stretch of the coast—from Cape Fear in North Carolina to St. Johns in north Florida—plantations that were able to use this highly productive method benefitted. (Courtesy of the Library of Congress.)

The rise and fall of the tide was integral in rice production. The water was needed to irrigate the fields throughout the growing season, which encouraged the growth of rice and controlled the weeds and pests. This entire process required constant attention by skilled slaves. Later, rice cultivation was affected by the Civil War and Reconstruction when planters found the necessary large workforce hard to come by. In the end, hurricanes in the late 1800s and early 20th century ended rice production in the South. (Courtesy of the Library of Congress.)

During the Colonial period, South Carolina and Georgia grew and amassed great wealth from the slave labor obtained from West Africa and coastal Sierra Leone. Forty percent of all America slaves passed through the Port of Charleston. Slaves from these regions commanded the highest prices due to their knowledge of growing rice. White planters put this knowledge to good use on the many rice plantations along South Carolina's coast. (Courtesy of the Library of Congress.)

The Africans were very knowledgeable about rice cultivation and taught the white plantation owners how to dike marshes and flood rice fields. The slaves milled rice by hand initially and then winnowed the rice in sweetgrass baskets—yet another skill the slaves brought with them from Africa. (Courtesy of the Library of Congress.)

With the advent of the rice mill, rice as a crop increased in profitability. Later in 1787, Jonathan Lucas introduced water power for the mills. Despite the increase in technology for the crop, the loss of slave labor sent the crops' profits spiraling down, never to recover. (Courtesy of the Library of Congress.)

apie (Indigo)

Introduction of indigo as a crop can be credited to the efforts of Eliza Lucas Pinckney. She received seeds from her father, who was governor of Antigua, with the thought that the crop might thrive in South Carolina. After several attempts, Pinckney had a successful crop in 1747 that was shipped to England. It was a staple crop of South Carolina until the Revolutionary War. (Courtesy of the Library of Congress.)

THE INDIGO MANUFACTORY
1 Vat. 2 Pounding Tub. 3 Receiver. 4 The Water filtrating from the Indigo 5 Indigo Plants. 6 Indians carrying 10 in Sacks 7 Drying Case 8 Indians carrying Indigo to the drying Case

Indigo reached its peak in 1773 when more than one million pounds of indigo was exported to England. During the Revolutionary War, the crop was neglected and attention was turned to rice. After the war, cheaper and better-quality indigo from India made it impossible for South Carolina to compete. Eventually, cotton became the main crop out of South Carolina. (Courtesy of the Library of Congress.)

The planting of sea island cotton began around 1786 along the sea islands of South Carolina and George by Barbadian cotton farmers that had come north. One of the earliest cotton planters was Francis Levett, who owned a Georgia plantation. He later fled Georgia at the outset of the American Revolution and settled in the Bahamas, where his attempts to produce cotton failed. (Courtesy of the Library of Congress.)

Due to its long staple (1.5 to 2.5 inches) and silky texture, sea island cotton received the highest price of all the cottons. It was often mixed with silk and used for the finest cotton counts. Eventually, it was eclipsed by upland cotton, which today makes up 95 percent of cotton produced in the United States. (Courtesy of the Library of Congress.)

Cotton remained an important crop in the South after emancipation. Free black farmers and white farmers continued to work on plantations as sharecroppers in return for a share of the profits. Reliable harvesting machines were developed eventually, and jobs in cotton faded away during the early 20th century. (Courtesy of the Library of Congress.)

Cotton requires plenty of sunshine, long periods without frost, and moderate rainfall to grow successfully. This crop works well in the dry tropics and subtropics of northern and southern hemispheres. Planting time in spring in the northern hemisphere ranges from the beginning of February to the beginning of June. Cotton is somewhat salt and drought tolerant; this makes it a great crop for arid and semiarid regions. (Courtesy of the Library of Congress.)

Cotton was a labor-intensive crop that required long days for slaves, usually about 12 hours working in the fields and even longer during harvest times. Both men and women worked in the cotton fields, as well as children. Children were considered half hands until they turned 12, at which time they were considered full hands. (Courtesy of the Library of Congress.)

A cotton gin is a machine that separates cotton fibers from their seeds quickly and easily, which had been a painstakingly slow job done by hand. Seeds must be removed to make the fibers usable, which when performed by hand took hundreds of man-hours to accomplish to gain a usable amount of lint. (Courtesy of the Library of Congress.)

Eli Whitney invented the first mechanical cotton gin in 1793. The machine used small wire hooks to pull cotton through a wire screen and had brushes that continuously removed loose cotton to prevent the apparatus from jamming. Automated cotton gins continued to be a crucial part of the modern cotton industry. (Courtesy of the Library of Congress.)

With Whitney's invention, 50 pounds of cotton could be cleaned in one day. By using a wooden cylinder that was surrounded by rows and rows of thin spikes, the cotton was pulled through grids that were closely spaced that prevented seeds from passing through. Loose cotton was brushed away so it did not cause the machine to jam. (Courtesy of the Library of Congress.)

The introduction of Whitney's cotton gin helped create a tremendously profitable crop that exploded in the South. The ease with which cotton could be cleaned increased production of the crop and helped to instigate expansion of the plantation system westward. It also increased the need for slave labor for the lucrative crop that made many fortunes throughout the South. (Courtesy of the Library of Congress.)

The expansion of cotton production rose from 750,000 bales in 1830 to 2.85 million bales in 1850. The resulting increase in production created a larger dependency for the South on the institution of slavery. The number of slaves also rose from 700,000 in 1790 to 3.2 million in 1850. By the Civil War, the South provided two-thirds of the world's cotton supply. (Courtesy of the Library of Congress.)

After the Civil War, a new workforce system called sharecropping evolved. Free black farmers worked on white-owned cotton plantations in return for a share of the profits from the sharecropper's yields. Vast labor forces were needed on cotton plantations to hand-pick cotton fibers, and it was not until the 1950s that reliable harvesting machinery was introduced into the South. As machines gradually replaced laborers, employment in the cotton industry fell. (Courtesy of the Library of Congress.)

Slave cabins varied from plantation to plantation. It is hard to know what the slave cabins of the Wadmalaw plantations looked like without actual photographs. It is possible to get an idea from slave cabins from other plantations, such as this interior shot of a slave cabin from Wormsloe, Isle of Hope, in Savannah, Georgia. These cabins show the darkness that most slave cabins retained as well as the quality of the furnishings. (Courtesy of the Library of Congress.)

Slave cabins on Wadmalaw plantations probably looked very much like the cabins found on Edisto Island. Usually made of wood with few windows, these cabins exemplified a common structure lived in by South Carolina slaves. (Courtesy of the Library of Congress.)

Cooking inside these windowless cabins would have been next to impossible during the hot summers. (Courtesy of the Library of Congress.)

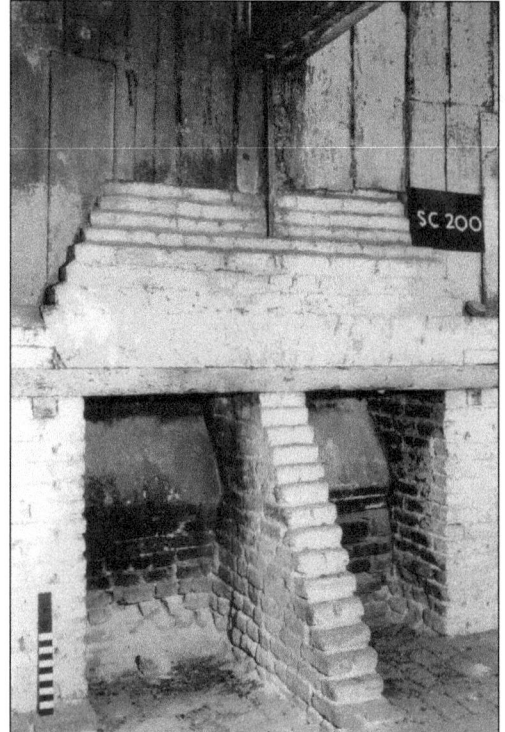

This slave cabin found in Hopsewee Plantation in Georgetown represents the tradition of more than one family living in a single slave cabin. A small divider can be seen indicating another wall that would have created two separate living spaces for two different families probably very similar to a modern duplex. (Courtesy of the Library of Congress.)

This 1936 photograph shows the interior of a slave cabin at Strawberry Hill Plantation in Greene County, Alabama. Many of these cabins were occupied through the middle of the 20th century. (Courtesy of the Library of Congress.)

Slave cabin designs varied from plantation to plantation and master to master. Some cabins were made of brick and used by slaves higher in the slave caste system, such as house servants and skilled slaves. Field hands would have been given the meanest of the cabins, probably windowless, wooden cabins with dirt floors such as these from Bass Place in Muscogee County, Georgia. (Courtesy of the Library of Congress.)

This style of cabin was probably used for field slaves. Windows are only found on the fronts of the cabins and do not allow for cross breezes. These cabins were often laid out into streets and could be found in different locations all over the plantation so that the slaves could be closer to the fields. (Courtesy of the Library of Congress.)

These basic cabins were found all over the South, even as far north as the Sotterly Plantation in St. Mary's County, Maryland. Only having a few windows may have been appreciated this far north, where there were more possibilities of drafts during the cold winter months. Summers would still have been hot in Maryland, and slaves would have found the cabins stifling in the heat. (Courtesy of the Library of Congress.)

Multifamily cabins were found on many other plantations, such as this cabin from the Cedars in Jefferson County, Missouri. Three separate doorways are found in these cabins, indicating they were used by three families sharing just one building. (Courtesy of the Library of Congress.)

This two-story cabin was photographed in St. Charles County, Missouri. The loft was likely where children of a large family slept. This cabin only has two windows—one on the first story and one on the second, allowing little opportunity for cross-ventilation in hot, oppressive Missouri summers. (Courtesy of the Library of Congress.)

This cabin from Hopsewee Plantation in Georgetown is intriguing in its use of African architectural aspects. The reflection of the African's heritage is indicative of the culture that many of the slaves were able to retain. The cultural influences that many of the slaves held on to can also be seen in the Gullah culture in the Lowcountry sea islands through their language, basket weaving, and quilts. (Courtesy of the Library of Congress.)

A unique slave cabin can be seen at the Arundel Plantation in Georgetown County, South Carolina. These slave cabins are nothing like the drab cabins of other plantations with many interesting architectural features such as arched windows and doorways. The plantation owner must have carried over his love of architectural detail throughout the buildings on his plantation. (Courtesy of the Library of Congress.)

The condition of many of these slave cabins did not change much after slavery ended. This 1936 photograph of a slave cabin and its resident was taken at the Barbara Plantation in St. Charles Parish, Louisiana. Instead of a door, the doorway has a sheet as a barrier. Later cabin owners did not invest much in improvements. They continued to live much as their ancestors did. (Courtesy of the Library of Congress.)

The word "Gullah" may have derived from the country of Angola, where many of the slaves were from. Others think it may have come from Native American words or from Gola, an ethnic group living in the border area between Sierra Leone and Liberia in West Africa, another area where many of the slaves would have come from. The word *Geechee*, another common name for the Gullah people, may have also come from an ethnic group living in the border area between Sierra Leone, Guinea, and Liberia called Kissi. (Courtesy of the Library of Congress.)

Most of the early slaves who created Gullah were brought through the ports of Charleston and Savannah as slaves. These slaves came from the West African rice-growing region, centered primarily in present-day Sierra Leone and through Bunce Island, the most significant port for slaves transported to the United States. The Gullah region once extended from southeast North Carolina to northeast Florida. (Courtesy of the Library of Congress.)

Gullahs were able to preserve much of their African culture because of geography, climate, and patterns of importation of enslaved Africans. The subtropical climate made the Lowcountry an excellent place for rice production, but it also made it vulnerable to the spread of malaria and yellow fever. Those tropical diseases, also endemic in Africa, were carried by slaves transported to the colonies by slave ships. Mosquitoes in the swamps and rice fields of the Lowcountry were able to pick up and spread the diseases to white planters. Malaria and yellow fever soon became endemic in the region. Africans were more resistant to these diseases since they were able to build immunity when they lived in Africa. (Courtesy of the Library of Congress.)

Planters devoted large areas of land to plantations for rice and indigo. As a result, the white population of the Lowcountry, especially the sea islands, grew at a slower rate than the black population. As more slaves were brought to the Lowcountry as the rice industry expanded, South Carolina eventually had a black majority be the early 1700s. Fearing disease, many white planters left the Lowcountry during the rainy spring and summer months when fever ran rampant and left these large groups of slaves isolated and not exposed to the white culture. (Courtesy of the Library of Congress.)

Planters would leave their African "rice drivers," or overseers, in charge of the plantations while they escaped the heat and disease of the plantation. The slaves were then able to retain their language and customs from working on large plantations with hundreds of other slaves, and the African traditions were also reinforced by new imports from the same regions. The slaves were able to develop a culture in which elements of African languages, cultures, and community life were preserved to a high degree. Their culture was very different from that of slaves in states like Virginia and North Carolina, where slaves lived in smaller settlements and had more interactions with whites. (Courtesy of the Library of Congress.)

During the Civil War, approximately 180,000 African Americans in 163 units served in the Union Army during the Civil War, and many more African Americans served in the Union Navy. These units were comprised of both free African Americans and runaway slaves and included men from all over the country. (Courtesy of the Library of Congress.)

On July 17, 1862, two acts were passed by Congress that allowed African Americans to enlist in the Army, but official enrollment did not start until after September and the issuance of the Emancipation Proclamation. It was generally thought by white soldiers and officers that black men did not have the courage to fight and fight well. After African American soldiers repelled Confederates at the battle of Island Mound, Missouri, in October, 1862, the critics were silenced. (Courtesy of the Library of Congress.)

Fourteen Negro regiments were in service by August 1863. In May 1863, at the battle of Port Hudson, Louisiana, African American soldiers made a brave advance over an open field toward deadly artillery fire. Their attack failed, but the African America soldiers proved they could withstand the stress of the heat of battle. (Courtesy of the Library of Congress.)

The most well-known battle fought by African American soldiers was the assault on Fort Wagner, South Carolina, by the 54th Massachusetts on July 18, 1863. The 54th volunteered to lead the assault against the strongly fortified Confederate positions. The soldiers of the 54th were successful at scaling the fort's parapet but were driven back after brutal hand-to-hand combat. (Courtesy of the Library of Congress.)

Although black soldiers proved themselves reputable soldiers over and over, they faced discrimination in their rate of pay and other areas. According to the Militia Act of 1862, soldiers of African descent were to receive $10 a month in pay, in comparison to $13 a month for white soldiers. Many regiments fought the inequality, and many refused to take any pay until finally on June 15, 1864, Congress granted equal pay for all black soldiers. (Courtesy of the Library of Congress.)

African American soldiers comprised 10 percent of the entire Union Army during the Civil War. Losses among African Americans were high, and from all reported casualties, approximately one-third of all African Americans enlisted in the Union Army died during the Civil War. (Courtesy of the Library of Congress.)

S | 21 | U.S.C.T.

Thomas Seabrook

, Co. *B*, 21 Reg't U.S. Col'd Inf.

Appears on

Company Descriptive Book

of the organization named above.

DESCRIPTION.

Age *28* years; height *5* feet *6* inches.

Complexion *Black*

Eyes *Black* ; hair *Black*

Where born *Wadmalaw, S.C.*

Occupation *Farmer*

ENLISTMENT.

When *Sept 28*, 186*4*.

Where *Hilton Head S.C.*

By whom *Lt. Davis* ; term *3* y'rs.

Remarks: *Credited to Dist. of Warwick, Orange Co. N.Y. Discharge for disability, at Mt. Pleasant S.C., May 29, 1865.*

J A Boyd

(383g) Copyist.

In September 1864, Thomas Seabrook enlisted in Hilton Head, South Carolina. He was born on Wadmalaw Island and was a 28-year-old who listed his occupation as a farmer. He is credited to District of Warwick Orange County, New York. Seabrook was discharged after an injury he sustained in Mount Pleasant, South Carolina, just north of Charleston, in May 1865. (National Archives and Record Administration.)

..............., Co..........., 34 Reg't U.S. Col'd

Appears on

Company Descriptive Book

of the organization named above.

DESCRIPTION.

Age *24* years; height *5* feet *10* inc

Complexion *Black*

Eyes *Black* ; hair *Black*

Where born *Wadmalaw Isl'd, S. C.*

Occupation *Field Hand*

ENLISTMENT.

When *Apr. 18*, 186

Where *Beaufort, S. C.*

By whom *Capt. Bryant* ; term *3* y

Remarks : *Deserted, (may 25 1863, Beaufort, S. C.*

Charles Fripp, a 24-year-old born on Wadmalaw Island, lists his occupation as a field hand. He enlisted in April 18, 1863, in Beaufort, South Carolina, and could have been an escaped slave from a nearby plantation. It is also listed that on May 25, 1863, Fripp deserted the Army in Beaufort. (National Archives and Record Administration.)

R | 34 | U.S.C.T.

William Rivers

, Co. *L*, 34 Reg't U.S. Col'd Inf.

Appears on

Company Descriptive Book

of the organization named above.

DESCRIPTION.

Age *25* years; height *5* feet *3* inches.

Complexion *Blk,*

Eyes *Blk*; hair *Blk.*

Where born *Wadmalaw Isl S. C,*

Occupation *Waiter,*

ENLISTMENT.

When *May 21*, 186 *3.*

Where *Beaufort,*

By whom *Capt. Bryant*; term *3* y'rs.

Remarks:

(383y)   Copyist.

William Rivers, another brave soul, was a 25-year-old black man born on Wadmalaw Island. His occupation is listed as "waiter," although it does not say where he was working at that time. Rivers enlisted in Beaufort, South Carolina, for a term of three years. (National Archives and Record Administration.)

M | 34 | U.S.C.T.

Peter Miller,

................, Co. _D_, 34 Reg't U.S. Col'd Inf.

Appears on

Company Descriptive Book

of the organization named above.

DESCRIPTION.

Age _24_ years; height _5_ feet _0_ inches.

Complexion _Blk_;

Eyes _Blk_; hair _Blk_.

Where born _Wadmalaw S.C._

Occupation _Laborer_.

ENLISTMENT.

When _24 mch_, 186_3_.

Where _Beaufort_

By whom _Capt Bryant_; term _3_ y'rs.

Remarks:

Pol

(383j)   Copyist.

Twenty-four-year-old Peter Miller was also born on Wadmalaw Island. He listed his occupation as "laborer." Since his occupation is not listed as a field hand, he may have been a free black or an escaped slave. He enlisted in Beaufort, South Carolina, for a term of three years. (National Archives and Record Administration.)

Three

ROCKVILLE

Maybank Highway, which runs from James Island through Johns Island, ends in Rockville on Wadmalaw Island. Rockville is located on Bohicket Creek, where legend has it local Indians would race canoes. Rockville is also home to the Annual Rockville Regatta held the first weekend of August since 1890. (Courtesy of the Charleston Public Library–Elias Ball Bull Collection.)

To escape the intense summer heat and the mysterious illness that accompanied Carolina summers, planters would often build seaside retreats for their families during the summer months. Not only were they able to relax by the cool, seaside beach, they were also out of reach of the seasonal malaria that infected many Lowcountry families. (Courtesy of the Charleston Public Library–Elias Ball Bull Collection.)

As these homes were built along the beaches, many villages sprang out of the construction. Planters found it easy to pack up their children, clothes, and furniture and relocate their social lives to these new little resorts. The ocean and nearby creeks also provided an abundance of seafood for families' enjoyment. ((Courtesy of the Charleston Public Library–Elias Ball Bull Collection.)

Rockville is one of Charleston County's oldest surviving summer resorts, dating to 1824. The architecture, transportation, and recreation of the town are important to the area, reflecting the same slow-moving lifestyle that the town has always been known for. (Courtesy of the Charleston Public Library–Elias Ball Bull Collection.)

Houses in Rockville fluctuate in size and level of architectural importance. Most all the houses have spacious porches, raised foundations, and large central hallways necessary for summer comfort. These houses have noticeable visual harmony. Like most houses in Charleston, homes in Rockville were designed to take full advantage of the sea breeze. (Courtesy of the Charleston Public Library–Elias Ball Bull Collection.)

Rockville was founded by Paul Hamilton, a man who received a 1,060-acre grant from King Charles II in 1736. The property was referred to as "The Rocks," or Rock Plantation, named after the rock deposits that run underneath Wadmalaw Island and jut out along the bluff of Rockville. (Courtesy of the Charleston Public Library–Elias Ball Bull Collection.)

The town is bordered to the south by Bohicket Creek, which for many years provided the main form of transportation for residents. Flat-bottomed ferry boats transported residents from a central wharf to other local islands or even into Charleston. Like the local Indians, residents also enjoyed racing homemade boats in the local creeks. (Courtesy of the Charleston Public Library– Elias Ball Bull Collection.)

Today, the little town of Rockville boasts 150 residents and has weathered many storms, hurricanes, and wars throughout the years. It has also retained the sleepy, slow-moving quality that helped define the town two almost centuries earlier. It also remains without tourist attractions or local retail establishments, staying almost completely untouched by current expansion. (Courtesy of the Charleston Public Library– Elias Ball Bull Collection.)

The clapboard house is believed to date before 1776, as it is included in a sale from Thomas Tucker to Benjamin Jenkins in December 1776. Jenkins also purchased the Rocks Plantation. The sale included Thomas Tucker's houses, buildings, land, and timber. (Courtesy of the Charleston Public Library–Elias Ball Bull Collection.)

Micah Jenkins later acquired this 1.5-story house. Jenkins was born in 1754 and was the nephew of Benjamin Jenkins. The house has a tabby basement with rooms that were once used as schoolrooms. The house was also used as offices for the Edisto Island Ferry Company. (Courtesy of the Charleston Public Library–Elias Ball Bull Collection.)

This home was owned by Sophia Sosnowski, who was the youngest daughter of Dr. Julius Christian Sosnowski of Bugby Plantation. Dr. Julius Sosnowski served as a doctor in the Confederacy during the Civil War. The Bugby Plantation remains in the Sosnowski family to this day. (Courtesy of the Charleston Public Library–Elias Ball Bull Collection.)

Sophia Sosnowski inherited the John F. Townsend home, where she lived in her adulthood. Sophia never married and eventually left the home to her niece, Sophia Seabrook Jenkins, daughter of Sophia's sister Mary Carolina Sosnowski Seabrook. In the event of Sophia Seabrook Jenkins's death, the house would then pass on to Sophia Sosnowski's grandnephew Rev. Frederick S. Sosnowski. (Courtesy of the Charleston Public Library–Elias Ball Bull Collection.)

The Agnes Wilkinson Wilson Windmill was named after the daughter of Edwards Girardeau and Mary Ida Warren Wilkinson. Agnes married Edwin Bates Wilson and had one child, Martha Mary Wilson. The windmill was installed around 1922 and supplied water to a residence. It is one of two such windmills in the Rockville area. (Courtesy of the Charleston Public Library–Elias Ball Bull Collection.)

This house displays the typical architecture of a Rockville summer home. Built in the late 19th century, the two-story wooden house sits on a large waterfront lot where it catches a refreshing breeze in the hot, humid summers. This was very helpful to those families that had escaped the stagnant plantations. (Courtesy of the Charleston Public Library–Elias Ball Bull Collection.)

Built by John Ferrars Sosnowski and Lena Washington LaRoche Sosnowski around 1897, the house was lived in by their daughter Grace Eudora Sosnowski and her husband, George Washington Seabrook. (Courtesy of the Charleston Public Library–Elias Ball Bull Collection.)

Built around
1853 by Edward
D. Bailey, this
two-story clapboard
house boasts six
Tuscan columns
with a first-floor
porch. Merle
Batson Whaley,
one of the most
memorable teachers
on Wadmalaw, lived
here and taught
fourth through
seventh grade to
the village children.
(Courtesy of the
Charleston Public
Library–Elias Ball
Bull Collection.)

The Maj. Daniel Jenkins House was built around 1834. It was named after the son of Benjamin and Elizabeth Jenkins (née Perry). Major Jenkins was the second occupant of the home after Gabriel and Ann Jenkins LaRoche Seabrook. (Courtesy of the Charleston Public Library–Elias Ball Bull Collection.)

The house was built in approximately 1843 by Gabriel Seabrook and his wife, Ann Jenkins LaRoche Seabrook. It was sold to Maj. Daniel Perry Jenkins, who passed it to his son Joseph Jenkins and his wife, Elizabeth Jenkins. The Jenkinses later left the house to their daughter, Elise Jenkins. (Courtesy of the Charleston Public Library–Elias Ball Bull Collection.)

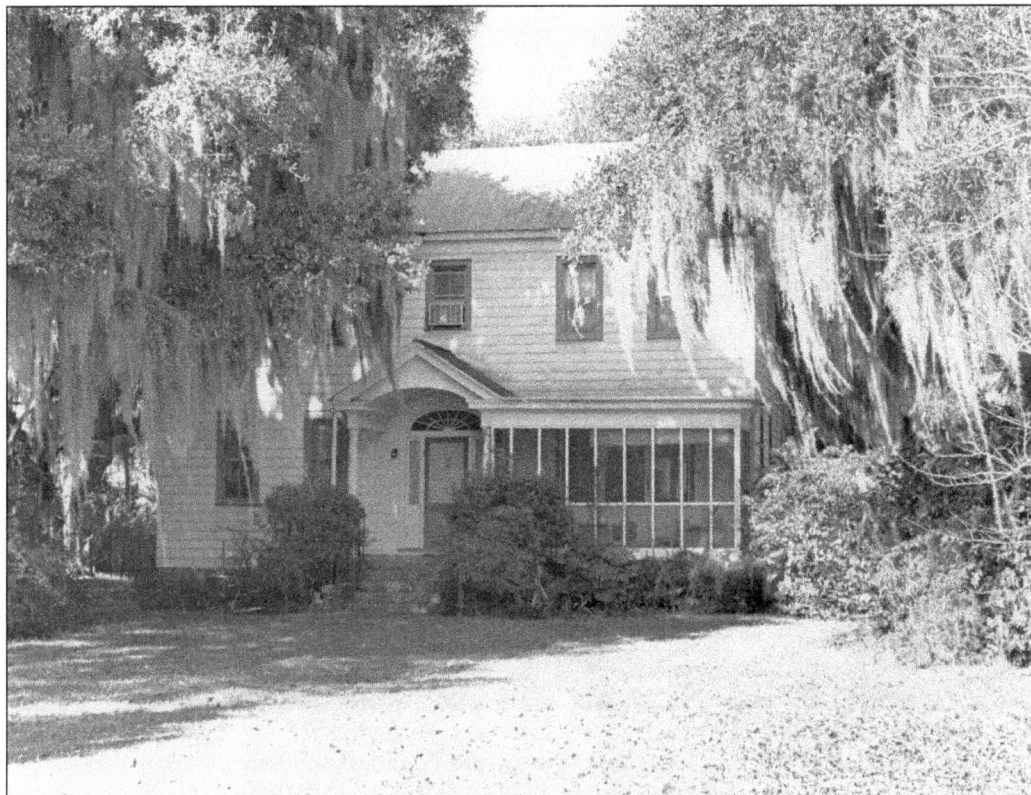

This house was built by Charles E. Fripp after he purchased the property in 1835 from John C. Wilson. The land previously was owned by William Seabrook of Edisto Island, then passed through several owners until it was purchased by William Hamilton Jenkins in the 1930s, who remodeled the house. (Courtesy of the Charleston Public Library–Elias Ball Bull Collection.)

This rectangular house is approximately three feet from the ground and has a single-story, one-room addition that runs the length of the house. The house itself is two stories tall and it stands on a half-acre lot behind the Episcopal rectory. (Courtesy of the Charleston Public Library–Elias Ball Bull Collection.)

Joseph Edings LaRoche built this house in 1835. He was married to Ella Murray LaRoche. The house originally sat on a tabby foundation, but in the 1930s it was lowered, which was unusual for a Rockville house. The house was intentionally built to maximize the amount of air and light through the windows. (Courtesy of the Charleston Public Library–Elias Ball Bull Collection.)

The Joseph Edings LaRoche house was next owned by Ned Seabrook and his wife, Susie Seabrook. Ned farmed at Jenkins Point on Johns Island and would row to the plantation every day, crossing Bohicket Creek to go to work on the neighboring island—a unique commute scenario. (Courtesy of the Charleston Public Library–Elias Ball Bull Collection.)

This house was originally one-third of a plantation house that stood near Orangeburg. It was first moved to a Johns Island plantation after the Civil War. In 1970, it was moved again to this waterfront lot, replacing a house that succumbed to a fire in 1969. (Courtesy of the Charleston Public Library–Elias Ball Bull Collection.)

The house was towed by two barges, the *Cornwallis* and the *Pocahontas*, from Exchange Plantation on Johns Island into Bohicket Creek off Wadmalaw Island. It is unknown what the original larger house at the Orangeburg Plantation looked like, but just this portion was enough to create a substantial house. (Courtesy of the Charleston Public Library–Elias Ball Bull Collection.)

The W.E. Jenkins house was built around 1838 for Dr. Edward M. Beckett by Edward D. Bailey. Bailey was a master builder known for his other homes in Rockville. Also known as the James LaRoche house, the summer home is high off the ground and boasts a three-sided porch to provide shade and catch necessary breezes in the summertime. The low roof also keeps inhabitants cool by preventing hot air from accumulating. (Courtesy of the Charleston Public Library–Elias Ball Bull Collection.)

Adm. George Palmer's Bridge, built around 1782, is one of only two brick bridges constructed before the Civil War in the Charleston area. The bridge is constructed of brick veneer in American bond, enclosing a fill mixture of crushed oyster shells and rammed earth. The original road was probably surfaced with a crushed-shell compound. The road was probably used for the commercial transportation of rice and indigo from plantation to market through the first quarter of the 19th century. By that time, the importance of these plantations on the sea islands was sharply declining. As a result, the road and bridge slowly fell into disuse. (Courtesy of the Charleston Public Library–Elias Ball Bull Collection.)

Four

WADMALAW CHURCHES

Many of the comforts of home were transplanted to these little villages by the sea—churches included. Rockville boasts two churches, Grace Episcopal Church and Rockville Presbyterian Church. Rockville Presbyterian Church, pictured here, resembles Charleston's St. Michael's Church because of its high steeple. It also has high steps, double-front doors, and pillars. (Courtesy of the Charleston Public Library–Elias Ball Bull Collection.)

Due to distance that must be traveled inland to other areas of the Lowcountry, it was not unusual for one church's minister to be absent on a Sunday. As both churches were Protestant, it was easy for either denomination to adapt to the other's service if its minister was kept away during the Sabbath. (Courtesy of the Charleston Public Library–Elias Ball Bull Collection.)

Grace Episcopal is a rectangular, wooden, one-story structure that is not high off the ground. The double-door entrance is Gothic in style with matching Gothic windows on either side. Four pillars with three-foot brick bases support the porch that extends along the entire width of the front of the church. The interior boasts brown wood stain and a small stained-glass window. (Courtesy of the Charleston Public Library–Elias Ball Bull Collection.)

A local parishioner, Dr. Daniel Jenkins Townsend, used slaves that were apprenticed in Charleston to build Rockville Presbyterian Church. (Courtesy of the Charleston Public Library–Elias Ball Bull Collection.)

This house was built in 1903 for Belle Crawford Seabrook. It was later used as the Presbyterian Manse for 26 years. Rev. Theodore Ashe Beckett and his family lived in the house for several years. The rectangular wooden house has brick pillars and is built three feet off the ground. (Courtesy of the Charleston Public Library–Elias Ball Bull Collection.)

The Episcopal rectory has been referred to as the most perfectly symmetrical house in Rockville. The front and back porches are matching as well as all the bays, the hipped roofs, and columns. (Courtesy of the Charleston Public Library–Elias Ball Bull Collection.)

The Rockville Presbyterian Church was built in the 1850s on part of the Rockland Plantation. Dr. Daniel Jenkins Townsend, who lived on Johns Island but spent his summers in the village of Rockville, owned the Rockland Plantation. He found it difficult to attend his usual church on Wadmalaw during the summers and therefore built the Rockville Presbyterian Church with the help of two of his slaves. Pictured is the front view of Rockville Presbyterian Church. (Courtesy of Kate Di Silvestre.)

Rockville Presbyterian Church, pictured from the back lawn, was designed in a style similar to many homes in Rockville. It was built 11 feet off the ground with pillars made of tabby, a mixture of shell and lime. The small, white church also has a long, wooden porch that extends the entire length of the church. The church also had a tall steeple. However, during the 1893 hurricane, the church's steeple was destroyed. Prior to being destroyed, the steeple was used as a lookout for boats in the North Edisto River during the Civil War. (Courtesy of Kate Di Silvestre.)

In June 2000, the Rockville Presbyterian Church introduced its Family Life Building. Inside are a modern kitchen, fellowship hall, office, and classroom. The building's design complements the historic church, despite being built in modern times. The building is located directly across the street from the church. (Courtesy of Kate Di Silvestre.)

New Bethlehem Baptist Church is the first building on Wadmalaw Island to have a fire sprinkler system. The 16,000-square-foot church, designed by Tim Latto, also has a full commercial kitchen and seating for approximately 500 people in both the sanctuary and fellowship hall. (Courtesy of Kate Di Silvestre.)

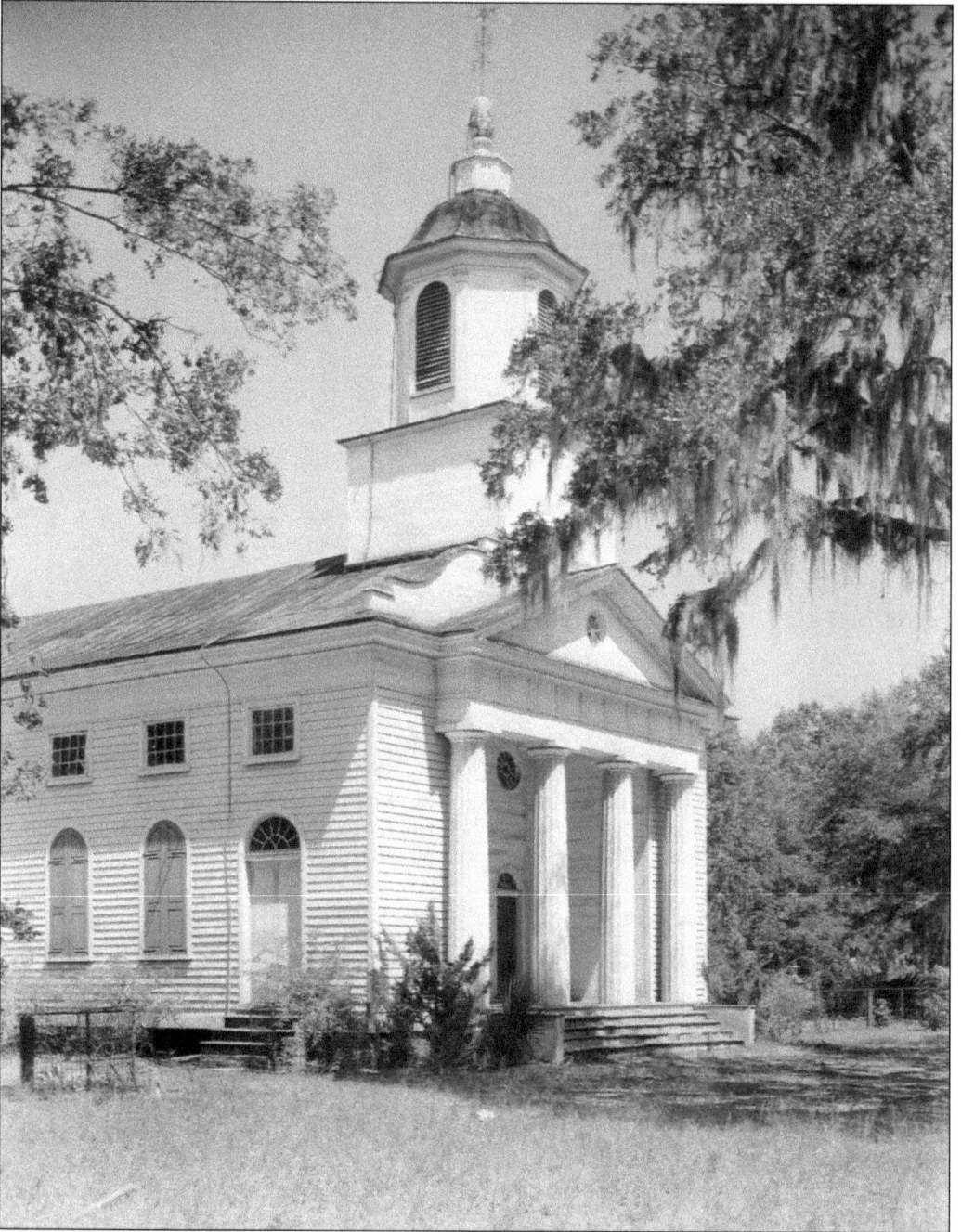

Churches were very important in the South, and almost all islands boasted a few. This grand structure is the Edisto Island Presbyterian Church and is very similar in size and design to the Presbyterian church found in Rockville. (Courtesy of the Library of Congress.)

Five

WADMALAW IN THE 20TH CENTURY

This photograph offers a glimpse at a time gone by. Pictured here are Sophia Seabrook, Maum Bessie, Claudia Seabrook, Grace Seabrook, and Oliver Seabrook. Many generations were raised by their nannies. The inclusion of the nanny in a picture showed that she played an important part in the family. (Courtesy of Lish Thompson.)

This is a photograph of Roger Mikell. He was a common sight selling his vegetables around the island and is a fond memory shared by many from the island. (Courtesy of Daisy Leland.)

Island children attended this old Wadmalaw schoolhouse. Good memories remain of the building, which was eventually torn down. Currently, the Leland Farms vegetable stand is there today. (Courtesy of Daisy Leland.)

James Clark Seabrook is pictured here on his horse. He was the owner of the Allandale Plantation. (Courtesy of Lish Thompson.)

This plantation house was James Clark's first home. Built in a Southern style with wide porches to catch the sea breeze, it was erected off the ground in a more typical farmhouse fashion. (Courtesy of Lish Thompson.)

James Clark's second home exhibited more of a plantation style featuring a broader home and wraparound porch. (Courtesy of Lish Thompson.)

Pictured are Oliver Frances Seabrook and Margaret "Peggy" Palmer Seabrook. Oliver was a well-known farmer, and Peggy was a Sunday school teacher. They were members of St. Johns Episcopal Church and had nine children. (Courtesy of Lish Thompson.)

The house at Allandale Plantation was photographed after a rare Christmas snow storm in 1989. This is the year of Hurricane Hugo in September, and many residents reported the unexpected weather change that accompanied the hurricane in the form of a snow that winter. (Courtesy of Lish Thompson.)

This image includes many generations of the family of Oliver Francis Seabrook on the steps of Allandale Plantation. (Courtesy of Lish Thompson.)

Wadmalaw resident Julia Hay Leland saved this multigenerational photograph of her family. (Courtesy of Daisy Leland.)

Grace Seabrook and Bess Bailey enjoy a day of fun in the sunshine aboard the *Undine* on Allandale Plantation. Boats were a common source of recreation and also an integral part of island life used as a main form of transportation into Charleston. (Courtesy of Lish Thompson.)

Grace Sosnowski Seabrook was a descendant of two well-known sea island families, the Sosnowskis, owners of Bugby Plantation, and the Seabrooks, who owned several plantations on Wadmalaw and nearby Edisto Island. (Courtesy of Lish Thompson.)

Leland Farms vegetable stand currently stands on the previous site of the Wadmalaw schoolhouse. Leland Farms is a local farm that helps provide the community with freshly grown produce and supports the purchase of locally grown foods. (Courtesy of Daisy Leland.)

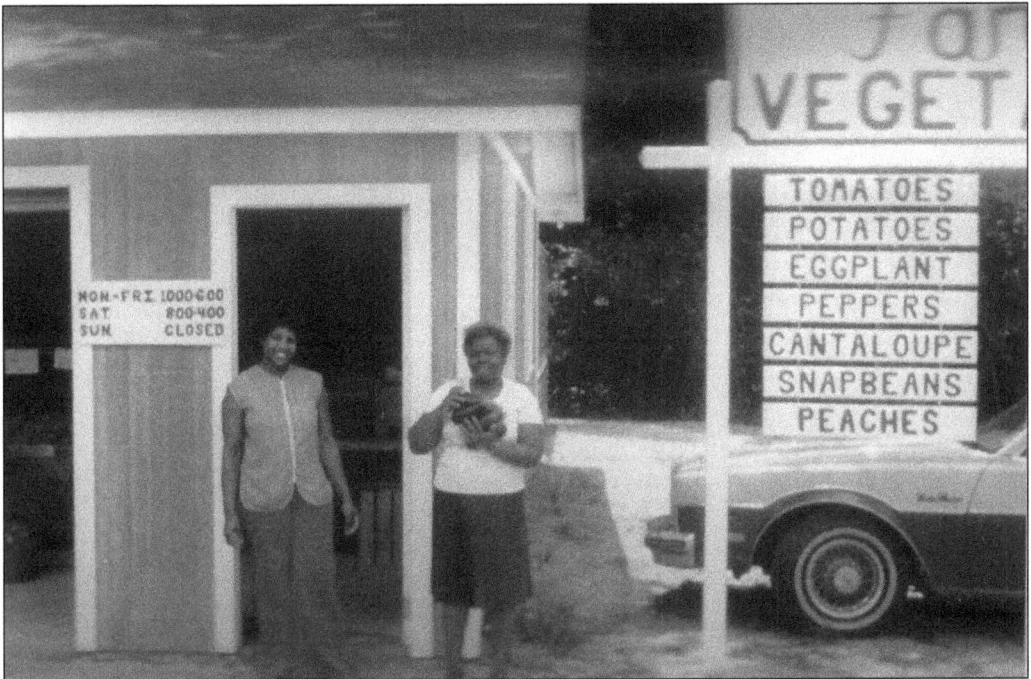

Leland Farms is a "U-Pick" farm that operates throughout the year. Blackberries are available late May through June. Blueberries, tomatoes, yellow and zucchini squash, bell peppers, slicing and pickling cucumbers, eggplant, green onions, as well as zinnias and cosmos are ready in June and July. (Courtesy of Daisy Leland.)

Pictured in 1982 are siblings Aaron M. Leland, Julie Leland Gervaise, and Kenneth W. Leland Jr. (Courtesy of Daisy Leland.)

Pictured here in 1982 are members of the Hay family of Wadmalaw, including Lewis H. Hay Jr., Julie Hay Leland, Henry M. Hay, Inez Hay James, Elizabeth Hay Mitchell, and Frank S. Hay. The group was celebrating Julia's 80th birthday. (Courtesy of Daisy Leland.)

The Seabrook dock is a reminder of days gone by. Transportation around the islands and to downtown Charleston was usually faster by boat than over land. This dock not only saw passengers but also was the point where crops would have been transported for sale. (Courtesy of Lish Thompson.)

The local Leland farms annual "U-Pick" always draws a crowd. Pictured picking strawberries are Richmond Wilhoit, Stephen Puckette, Erin Leland, Elizabeth Puckette, and Eliza Drayton Wilhoit. (Courtesy of Lish Thompson.)

Many generations passed their lifetimes on Wadmalaw Island. James Clark Seabrook, seated on the steps of Allandale Plantation, is one of the many folks who lived his life out on the island. (Courtesy of Lish Thompson.)

In 1989, Hurricane Hugo blew through Charleston. Most of the damage was found in the northern part of the county, but even Wadmalaw on the southern end had its share of damage. Many boats, like the ones seen here, were tossed up out of the water onto land. (Courtesy of Lish Thompson.)

Wadmalaw is also home to the New Cut Plantation Triathlon. Wadmalaw is the perfect setting for outdoor events like this. (Courtesy of Elizabeth "Libby" Leland Puckette.)

These creeks are on the property of Selkirk Plantation. (Courtesy of Lish Thompson.)

Leadenwah Creek was part of an important system of waterways that planters relied on. Over land, travel to Charleston took a very long time; the time could be cut immensely by use of the creeks to the ocean. This was a great way for planters to transport their crops to sell. (Courtesy of Lish Thompson.)

Adm. Richard Wilder "Dick" Smith and his wife, Elenora "Ellen" Irene Septima Natalie Sellars Smith, lived on Wadmalaw Island during the 1960s and 1970s. Dick built the house and did all the wiring. He learned electrical systems during his time training in the Navy. Elenora was the most cosmopolitan of her family.

A funny family story of the Smiths involves the mail and their dog. Ellen and Dick's nephew would send letters addressed to "Davey the dog, Wadmalaw Island, SC." That was it for the address. Everyone on Wadmalaw knew their dog, so the postman would deliver letters at the house for Davey. Their nephew kept an ongoing correspondence with Davey for years (his aunt wrote the letters in response). Davey was treated like the child that Ellen and Dick never had.

Six

WADMALAW TODAY

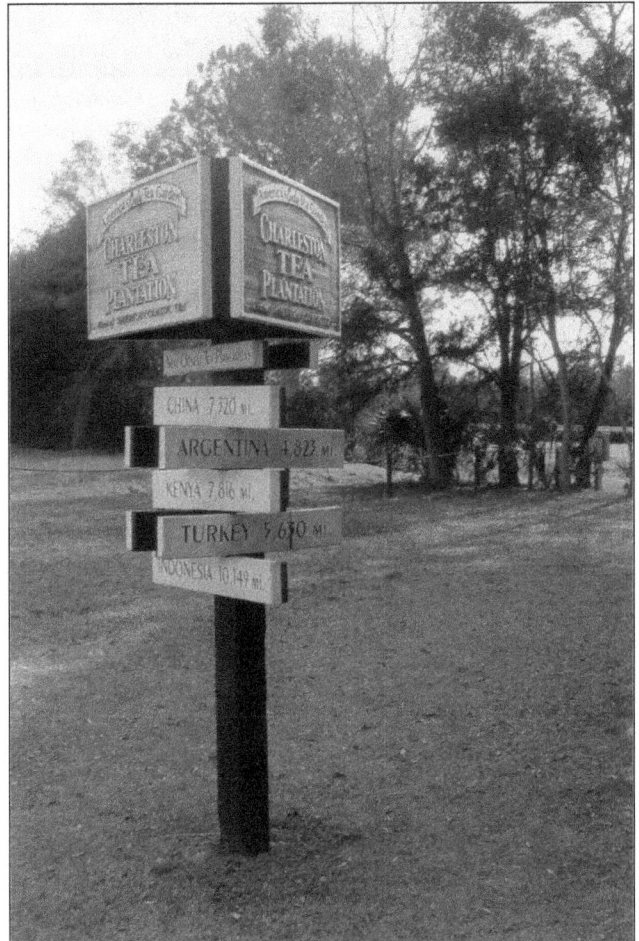

Wadmalaw Island is home to America's only commercial tea garden, the Charleston Tea Plantation. Wadmalaw Island provides an idyllic environment for growing tea thanks to the island's sandy soils, subtropical climate, and the approximate 52 inches of rainfall the island receives each year. (Courtesy of the Charleston Tea Plantation.)

The Charleston Tea Plantation has 127 acres of *Camellia sinensis* tea plants that are used to produce black and green teas. More than 320 varieties are located on the Charleston Tea Plantation grounds, home to both a working tea factory (pictured) and a gift shop. (Courtesy of the Charleston Tea Plantation.)

The history of the Charleston Tea Plantation dates back to the 1700s when the *Camellia sinensis* plant (pictured) first arrived in the United States from China. Throughout the next 150 years, there were several attempts to propagate and produce tea from this tea plant for consumption. However, none of the attempts were successful until 1888 when Dr. Charles Shepard founded the Pinehurst Tea Plantation in Summerville, South Carolina. Dr. Shepard continued to propagate and produce award-winning teas for consumption until his death in 1915. In 1960, the Thomas J. Lipton Company purchased the Pinehurst Tea Plantation, which had been abandoned following Dr. Shepard's death. (Courtesy of the Charleston Tea Plantation.)

Thomas Lipton moved the surviving *Camellia sinensis* tea plants to a 127-acre potato farm on Wadmalaw Island. For 24 years following the transplant, the farm was used as a research center. There, Mack Fleming, a horticulturist who was in charge of the operation, decided because of the unstable climate and high labor costs in South Carolina, that tea production there was unfeasible. (Courtesy of Kate Di Silvestre.)

In 2003, the Bigelow family formed a partnership with Hall and purchased the Charleston Tea Plantation at auction. The Bigelow family is committed to protecting the planet and improving the community. They do not use any herbicides, fungicides, or insecticides on their tea plants. In addition, the tea plantation has a custom-made irrigation system that allows the plants to be watered solely off of rain and pond water. They also use tea waste—the stems and fibers of made tea—as mulch to fertilize the tea plants. (Courtesy of Kate Di Silvestre.)

The plantation is open year-round, seven days a week to the public. Guests can enjoy an informative factory tour that is narrated by Hall, a trolley tour of the tea grounds, and sample some of the American Classic Tea. The grounds also have a gift shop where they can purchase a variety of flavored black teas, including peach, raspberry, and a Charleston blend, as well as green tea. Both loose-leaf teas and pyramid teas can be purchased. (Courtesy of Kate Di Silvestre.)

The Charleston Tea Plantation is also a popular location for events. People can have their wedding at the plantation, host a family reunion, or have a corporate meeting or event with a backdrop of the tea plants and live oaks. Pictured is a field of *Camellia sinensis* tea plants and a tea picker. (Courtesy of Kate Di Silvestre.)

The plantation also hosts an annual First Flush Festival. The festival is a celebration of the tea plantation and the plantation's American Classic Tea. "First flush" refers to the new growth of leaves on the *Camellia sinensis* tea plants in the springtime. The result of the new leaves is the freshest cup of tea possible. The festival also has music, entertainment, art, and local cuisine for the local residents to enjoy. (Courtesy of Kate Di Silvestre.)

Wadmalaw Island is home to Charleston's only winery, Irvin~House Vineyards. The vineyard is situated on 48 acres of a former carriage company's property. The ground is home to a winery and tasting room, a renovated party barn, flower and vegetable gardens, chicken coops, and a picnic area. (Courtesy of Kate Di Silvestre.)

When Jim and Ann Irvin retired, their shared love of gardening and Jim's lifelong desire to make wine led them to their Wadmalaw Island property. In 2001, the Irvins purchased and planted 2,700 grape vines on seven-and-a-half miles of trellis. Irvin~House wine is made specifically from muscadine grapes, the only grape that will grow in South Carolina's humid climate. (Courtesy of Irvin~House Vineyards.)

Irvin~House Vineyards produces an array of white and red wines from their grapes. These wines include Tara Gold, a semidry, mellow white table wine; Magnolia, a sweet, fruity white wine; Live Oak reserve, a blend of soft, subtle fruit flavors; Mullet Hall Red, a dry, red table wine with a lively fruity flavor; and Palmetto, a sweet, rich, light-bodied fruity muscadine flavor. (Courtesy of Irvin~House Vineyards.)

The Irvins decided to use the work of local artists to create the labels for their bottles. Five Charleston-area artists were selected, including William Jameson for the Tara Gold label; Mark Horton for the Mullet Hall Red label; Charlynn Knight for the Magnolia label; Matt Constantine for the Palmetto label; and Hilarie Lambert for the Live Oak Reserve label. (Courtesy of Irvin~House Vineyards.)

The Firefly Distillery is located on the same property as Irvin~House Vineyards on Wadmalaw Island. Jim Irvin, owner of Irvin~House Vineyards with his wife, Ann, teamed up with Scott Newitt, who was the manager of a local liquor distributor to create Firefly Vodka, a vodka company that utilizes Irvin's muscadine grapes. (Courtesy of Firefly Vodka.)

The Firefly Distillery now produces several flavors of vodka in addition to the original sweet tea vodka. This includes raspberry, lemon, mint, peach, and a "skinny" version. The company also makes sweet tea bourbon, straight vodka, and Southern lemonade vodka. (Courtesy of Kate Di Silvestre.)

In 1931, Camp Ho Non Wah got its start when the Coastal Carolina Council held its first summer Boy Scout Camp on the Bailey family's plantation. The plantation is located on Wadmalaw Island along the shore of the Bohicket River. The Boy Scouts camped in front of the Baileys' original home, cooked in patrols, and swam in the small swimming hole on the property. Due to the success of the first program, the Bailey family arranged for the camp to be held on its property each summer. (Courtesy of Camp Ho Non Wah.)

In 1932, the camp was named Camp Ho Non Wah, meaning "the land of rising and falling waters." Over the coming years, the Coastal Boys Council secured more land around Ho Non Wah allowing room for a new dining hall to be built in the 1930s. In addition, the first established campsite area was cleared and equipped with Adirondack cabins.

Over the years, several other renovations were completed on Camp Ho Non Wah, including a 1946 renovation where the swimming hole was replaced with a swimming pool. In 1951, a nature lodge was built, and in 1957 the pageant grounds were built, which is now called the Council Ring. Pictured is the camp's chapel. (Courtesy of Camp Ho Non Wah.)

In 1959, Hurricane Grace hit Camp Ho Non Wah, tearing off the second floor of the Bailey family's home (pictured). Renovations have taken place in order to restore the Bailey family home. In addition, a major renovation taking place between 1981–1985 provided campers with a new dining hall, trading post, and staff center. (Courtesy of Camp Ho Non Wah.)

The camp offers aquatics facilities; an archery, rifle, and shotgun range; a handicraft shelter; an ecology lodge; a Scout craft shelter, over 13 miles of hiking trails; a natural amphitheater with sound system; an air-conditioned dining hall; trading post; and Scoutmaster lodge. Pictured are campers gathering at a morning assembly at the camp, where the flags are raised and camp-wide announcements are shared with the troops. Ho Non Wah also has troop-sized campsites in 14 different locations. Each of the campsites comes equipped with two-man tents, a latrine, and a washing station. (Courtesy of Camp Ho Non Wah.)

Pictured is the ranger's house at Camp Ho Non Wah. The camp offers both summer and winter camps where Boy Scouts can earn merits in such programs as American cultures, archery, lifesaving, astronomy, mammal study, nature, oceanography, rowing, Scouting heritage, reptile and amphibian study, and small boat sailing. (Courtesy of Kate Di Silvestre.)

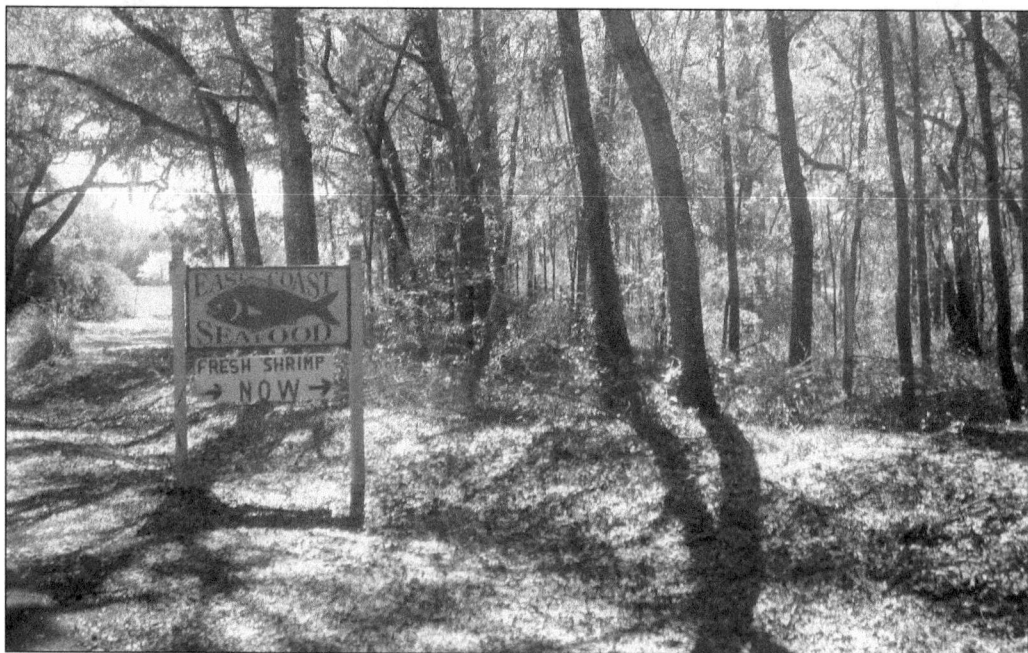

East Coast Seafood Company is located near the end of Cherry Point Road, right before the Cherry Point Boat Landing on Wadmalaw Island. Local Jimmy Green owns East Coast Seafood Company. The company sells fresh shrimp and fish right off the boat on a daily basis to both area restaurants and local residents. (Courtesy of Kate Di Silvestre.)

Cherry Point Seafood Company is located at the end of Cherry Point Road on Wadmalaw Island. Micah LaRoche is the local, longtime owner of the Cherry Point Seafood Company. The company sells fresh shrimp and other fish right off the boat to local residents, restaurants, and the general public. (Courtesy of Kate Di Silvestre.)

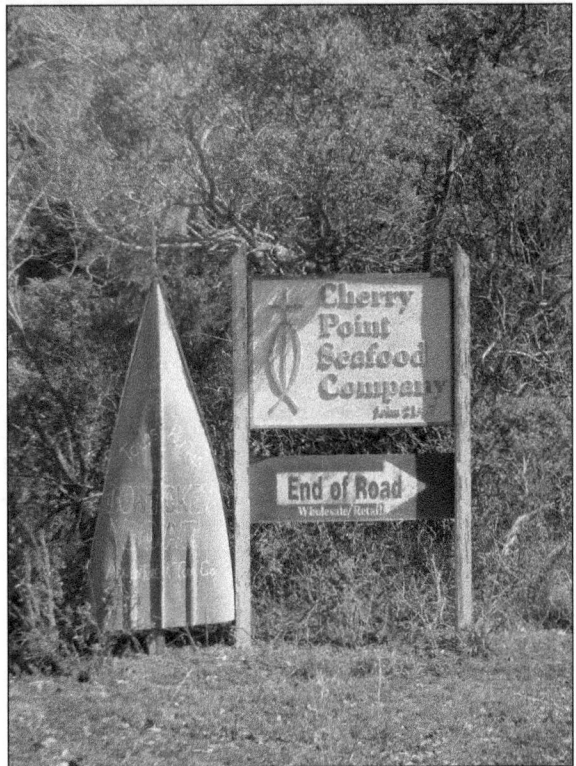

Pictured is the Cherry Point Seafood sign. Area shrimp trawlers pay to dock their boats and ice their shrimp and catch. Inside Cherry Point Seafood Company is a sorting room with packing and storage facilities available for use. Many of the boats that pay to dock are transient boats that depend upon seafood companies such as Cherry Point for support during the shrimping season. (Courtesy of Kate Di Silvestre.)

This view is from the Cherry Point Boat Landing, the only public boat landing on Wadmalaw Island. It is located in Bohicket Creek. Shrimp boats can often be seen from the landing as they move into and dock at Cherry Point Seafood Company. (Courtesy of Kate Di Silvestre.)

Wadmalaw Island boasts an active community center. The center was organized in 1962, but it was moved to its current location (pictured) in October 1982. Members of the Wadmalaw Island Citizen Improvement Council host many events here at the community center for local residents, including jewelry making, knitting classes, and Zumba classes. (Courtesy of Kate Di Silvestre.)

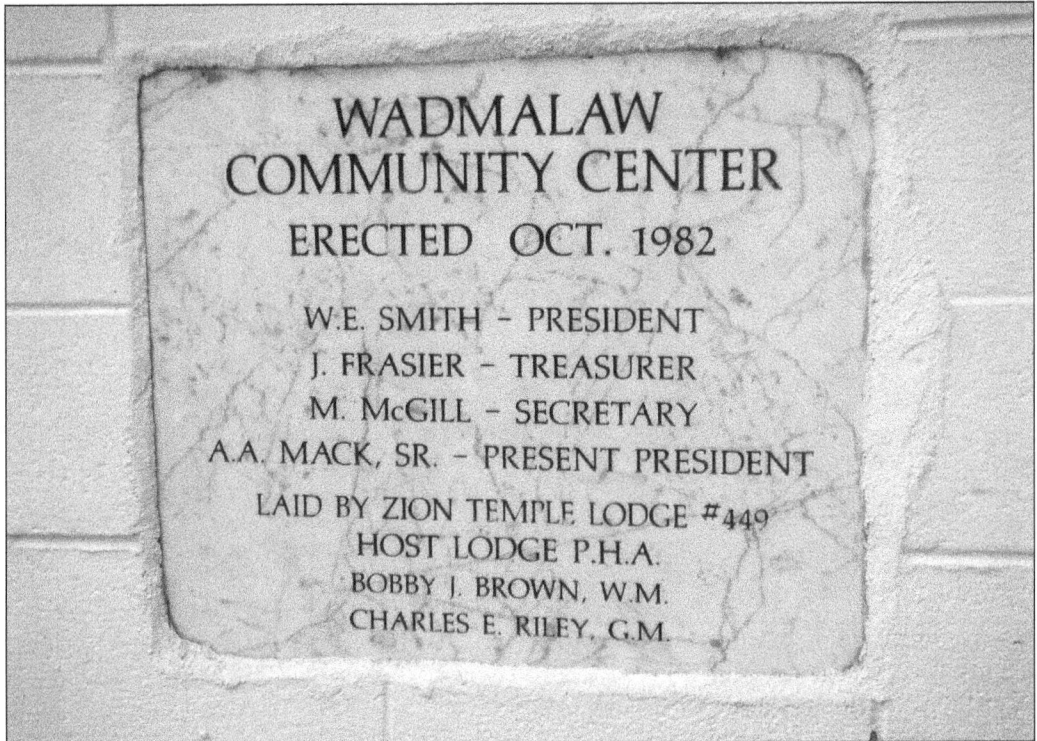

This plaque is built into the wall of the new Wadmalaw Island Community Center building. It reads, "Erected Oct. 1982; W.E. Smith – President, J. Frasier – Treasurer, M. McGill – Secretary, A.A. Mack, Sr. – Present President; Laid by Zion Temple Lodge #449, Host Lodge P.H.A., Bobby J. Brown, W.M., Charles E. Riley, G.M." (Courtesy of Kate Di Silvestre.)

The Wadmalaw Island Community Center, located at 5605 Katy Road off Maybank Highway, hosts various events including spaghetti dinners and hosts a Gullah celebration. The celebration features Gullah cuisine, Gullah storytelling, local arts and crafts, and gospel singing. Pictured is the Wadmalaw Island Community Center sign, located at the entrance of Katy Road. (Courtesy of Kate Di Silvestre.)

Thelma Smalls Davis, who lives in Wadmalaw six months per year and in Italy the other six months per year, teaches other Wadmalaw Island residents how to make their own jewelry at the Wadmalaw Community Center. She is pictured with (from left to right) Alice LaRoche, Mamie Mack, and Henrietta Barnette, who are all local Wadmalaw residents. (Courtesy of the Wadmalaw Island Citizen Improvement Committee.)

Each year since 1999, the community center has put on an annual Labor Day festival for residents. During the festival, locals cook, eat, mingle, and enjoy the Labor Day parade. Pictured is the St. James AME Church, whose members decorated their float and participated in the Labor Day parade alongside other Wadmalaw churches. (Courtesy of the Wadmalaw Island Citizen Improvement Committee.)

Local Wadmalaw residents enjoy the 11th-annual Labor Day parade, food, and festivities held September 6, 2010. Pictured seated (from left to right) are Isaiah Vance, John Mitchell, and Don Adams. Pictured standing are Melvin Hunter, Leroy Linen, and Francis Linen. (Courtesy of Wadmalaw Island Citizen Improvement Committee.)

In 1905, the Sea Island Yacht Club organized when the *Undine* of Wadmalaw Island and the *Lizzie B.* of James Island raced one another. A purpose of the organization was to promote amateur sailboat racing and to bring together the people of the area's sea islands. The organization is still open today. (Courtesy of Kate Di Silvestre.)

The annual sailboat race is the oldest on the East Coast and is really like a giant party on the water. The two-day race takes place on a mile-long stretch of Bohicket Creek and usually gathers a crowd of about 400 people. Attendees often raft their sailboats together and float the days away alongside the banks while they watch the race nearby. (Courtesy of Beardan Barnes.)

The Rockville Regatta started out as a family-friendly competition between island residents 120 years ago. It began when Confederate veterans converged on Rockville for a reunion. The veterans enjoyed the village and eventually started bringing their families with them for the reunion and used it as a vacation spot where they could swim and sail as a reunion of sorts. (Courtesy of Beardan Barnes.)

Eventually, an actual race or regatta started to evolve and was held annually the first week in August after the summer harvest. Bohicket Creek was perfect for racing with a fast current. Local legend includes stories of Indian tribes using it to race their canoes. The race is first mentioned in 1842, with the first official regatta held in 1890 when two cousins, John F. Sosnowski and Jenkins Mikell, raced for bragging rights. (Courtesy of Beardan Barnes.)

The Sea Island Yacht Club is also the home of the Sea Island One Design on Wadmalaw Island. The Sea Island One Design was first designed to sail in the Rockville Regatta and eventually inspired other local yacht club members to build their own designs and to establish their own invitational regatta. Since World War II, this design is native to the waterways in and around Charleston, where it has been the main event at Rockville since its design. (Courtesy of Beardan Barnes.)

The shrimping industry has a long history in the Lowcountry. From 1850 to 1940, shrimpers included the "Mosquito Fleet" manned by African Americans. They would sell their catch by peddling the shrimp via cart through the streets of Charleston. The Mosquito Fleet sailed for almost 100 years, but shrimping by sail ended in 1940. (Courtesy of Library of Congress.)

Before World War II, the first shrimp-packing house opened in Port Royal in 1924. The first cannery followed in Beaufort in 1928. During the war, the industry declined along with canning. Fresh shrimp shipped by truck became standard in 1948. Boat building grew in Florida, North Carolina, and parts of South Carolina with larger, stronger craft being constructed. (Courtesy of Library of Congress.)

Since the 1970s, the shrimping market has changed. Shrimp is no longer a luxury product and the public demand outweighs domestic production, causing an increase of imported shrimp to enter the market. High fuel costs have also caused the shrimping industry to decline. Several organizations have formed to help local shrimpers, such as the South Carolina Seafood Alliance and Wild American Shrimp, Inc. (Courtesy of the Library of Congress.)

An old sea buoy now lies in front of Rockville Presbyterian Church's Family Life Building. Sea buoys have several purposes for fisherman, including marking areas that allow boats to navigate safely, as a lifebuoy, or to identify traps. (Courtesy of Kate Di Silvestre.)

Martin's Point plantation is probably the most famous of the plantations on Wadmalaw Island. It is most famously known for being in the movie *The Notebook*, which was filmed in the Charleston area in 2004. The plantation was the home of the character Noah and was a focal point of the film. (Courtesy of Tristan Rosier)

Many movies were filmed in Wadmalaw. *Paradise* (1991) portrays a young couple torn apart by a family tragedy. Their marriage is saved when a young boy visits. (Courtesy of Lish Thompson.)

Another recent television movie, *The* Hunley, tells the true story of the *H.L. Hunley* submarine and the battle that happened on February 17, 1864, in Charleston Harbor. The movie starred Armand Assante, Donald Sutherland, Alex Jennings, Michael Dolan, and Christopher Bauer. (Courtesy of Lish Thompson.)

Visit us at
arcadiapublishing.com